Meg
Cailín

IRISH
PROVERBS

Over 200 Insightful Proverbs
in 15 Categories

Jean LeGrande

Happy
26th birthday
with love from
mom + all
your Irish
ancestors, +
Gaelic
the cat !

Other Books from Jean LeGrand:

Irish Dinner
Irish Treats
Irish Drinks
Irish Toasts
Irish Blessings
Irish Curses

Published by
FastForwardPublishing.com

ISBN-13: 978-1499258356
ISBN-10: 1499258356

A SURPRISE GIFT

To say "Thanks" for buying this book, I would like to give you
a FREE COPY of my book
IRISH CURSES - Over 100 Traditional Irish Curses ...

Get Your Free Book Here:
http://www.fastforwardpublishing.com/Thank-You-Irish-Curses.html

TABLE OF CONTENTS

DEDICATION

This book is dedicated to Kevin Michael McGrath, a true renaissance man who is a skilled musician that can bring a crowd to its feet or a room to tears with his traditional Irish bag pipes."All the other instruments I play are accompaniment," says McGrath. "On the other hand, the Uilleann Pipes are an extension of me. It's a direct transfer of spiritual and emotional expression."

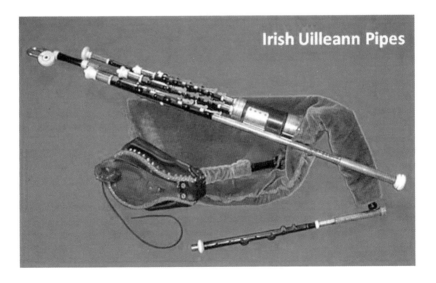

Irish Uilleann Pipes

Unlike the better known Scottish Great Highland pipes which were historically played outdoors (and primarily on the battlefield), the Uilleann Pipes (the traditional Irish bagpipes) are made to play music indoors and are notably quieter and sweeter in tone. And, the Scottish Great Highland pipes (also known as the Great Irish Warpipes) are inflated when the player blows into the bag, while the Uilleann Pipes are inflated by a small set of bellows held under the player's arm.

IΠTRODUCTIOΠ

A proverb is a concise and simple statement that expresses a common sense truth. It is popularly known and repeated. With their rich history in written and spoken language, the Irish are recognized as a source for many proverbs that effectively express commonplace truth and useful thought.

In this book you will find over 200 Irish Proverbs that you can use for inspiration, motivation, to offer advice or to clarify a point in either a personal or a business situation. Some are profound. Some are funny.

You will probably commit one or two to memory and find, that when used at the right time can have a profoundly positive impact on your communication. Enjoy.

Irish Proverbs
CHARACTER & HONOR

Better good manners than good looks.

It is more difficult to maintain honor than to become prosperous.

Promise is in honor's debt.

Forgetting a debt doesn't mean it's paid

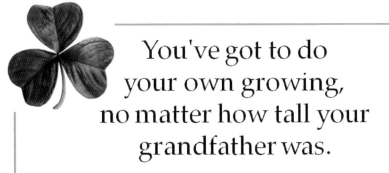

You've got to do
your own growing,
no matter how tall your
grandfather was.

A man may live after losing his life but not after losing his honor.

Better to be a man of character than a man of means.

If you dig a grave for others you may fall into it yourself.

If you don't want flour on your clothes, stay out of the mill.

Even a tin knocker will shine on a dirty door.

The friend that can be bought is not worth buying.

An oak is often split by a wedge from its own branch.

A good retreat is better than a bad stand.

The light heart lives long.

The hole is more honorable than the patch.

A friend's eye is a good mirror.

It's no use carrying an umbrella if your shoes are leaking.

It's no use boiling your cabbage twice

Every man's mind is his kingdom.

Better the trouble that follows death than the trouble that follows shame.

If you come up in this world be sure not to go down in the next.

Who gossips with you will gossip of you.

Lie down with dogs and you'll rise with fleas.

Farfad Lighthouse

Irish Proverbs
OPPORTUNITY

You'll never plough a field by turning it over in your mind.

You won't learn to swim on the kitchen floor.

Slow is every foot on an unknown path.

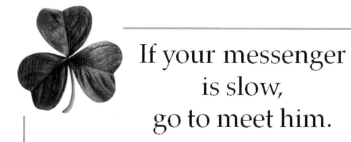

If your messenger
is slow,
go to meet him.

There are fish in the sea better than have ever been caught.

A combed head sells the feet.

Don't make little of your dish for it may be an ignorant fellow who judges it.

Many a sudden change takes place on an unlikely day.

Irish Proverbs
HUMAN NATURE

Everyone lays a burden on the willing horse.

Instinct is stronger than upbringing.

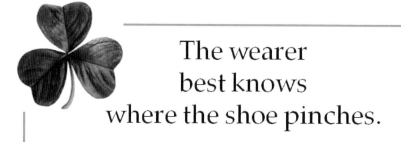

The wearer
best knows
where the shoe pinches.

Both your friend and your enemy think you will never die.

The well fed does not understand the lean.

A man without dinner— two for supper.

Men are like bagpipes - no sound comes from them until they are full.

He who comes with a story to you brings two away from you.

You never miss the water till the well runs dry.

Everyone feels his own wound first.

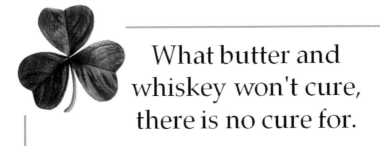

What butter and whiskey won't cure, there is no cure for.

The pig in the sty doesn't know the pig going along the road.

Pity him who makes an opinion a certainty.

No two people ever lit a fire without disagreeing.

Seeing is believing, but feeling is the God's own truth.

A glowing gríosach (ember) is easily rekindled.

The person bringing good news knocks boldly on the door.

Baltimore Beacon

Irish Proverbs
PATIENCE

God made time, but man made haste.

The raggy colt often made a powerful horse.

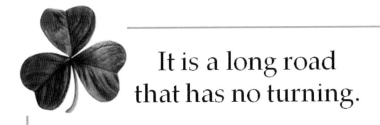

It is a long road that has no turning.

It takes time to build castles. Rome wan not built in a day.

Patience is poultice for all wounds.

When the apple is ripe it will fall.

The mills of God grind slowly but they grind finely.

If you do not sow in the spring you will not reap in the autumn.

Never dread the winter till the snow is on the blanket.

The day will come when the cow will have use for her tail.

Time and patience would bring a snail to America.

When a twig grows hard it is difficult to twist it. Every beginning is weak.

Clonmacnoise

Irish Proverbs
STUPIDITY

A man with no wit has little on a pig.

The world would not make a racehorse of a donkey.

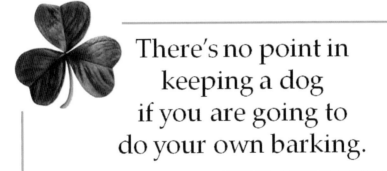

There's no point in
keeping a dog
if you are going to
do your own barking.

You may as well give cherries to a pig as advice to a fool.

Only a fool burns his coal without warming himself.

Stupidity is sending the goose on a mission to the fox's den.

There are two things that cannot be cured: death and the want of sense.

Irish Proverbs
WISDOM

Three best to have in plenty - sunshine, wisdom and generosity.

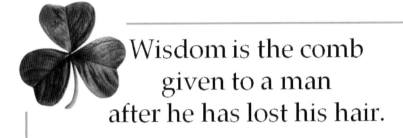

Wisdom is the comb
given to a man
after he has lost his hair.

Though wisdom is good in the beginning, it is better at the end.

The fear of God is the beginning of wisdom.

Dublin Castle

Irish Proverbs
DRINKING

A man takes a drink, the drink takes a drink, the drink takes the man.

It's the first drop that destroys you, there's no harm at all in the last.

The truth comes out when the spirit goes in.

Good as drink is,
it ends in thirst.

If it's drowning you're after, don't torment yourself with shallow water.

A drink precedes a story.

Thirst is the end of drinking and sorrow is the end of drunkenness

It is sweet to drink but bitter to pay for.

When the drop (drink) is inside, the sense is outside.

When the liquor was gone the fun was gone.

Wine divulges truth.

Old Ireland House

Irish Proverbs
ADVICE

Blow not on dead embers.

Never bolt your door with a boiled carrot.

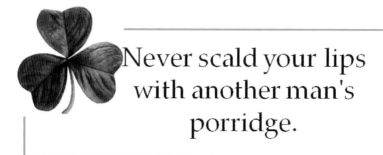

Never scald your lips with another man's porridge.

Listen to the sound of the river and you will get a trout.

A nod is as good as a wink to a blind horse.

God is good but don't dance in a currach (small boat).

What butter and whiskey won't cure, there is no cure for.

Beware an Irishman who loves his wife the most but his mother the longest.

A man without a blackthorn stick is a man without an expedient.

Be neither intimate nor distant with the clergy.

Never sell a hen on a wet day.

Never reach out your hand further than you can withdraw it.

Show the fatted calf, but not the thing that fattened him.

National University of Galway

Irish Proverbs
WORK & IDLENESS

A bad workman quarrels with his tools.

It's a dirty bird that won't keep its own nest clean.

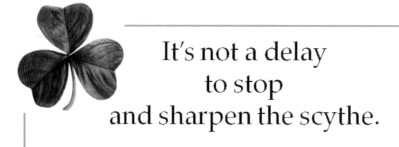

It's not a delay
to stop
and sharpen the scythe.

There is no luck except where there is discipline.

Keep your shop and your shop will keep you.

It is the good horse that draws its own cart.

The man who has luck in the morning has luck in the afternoon.

He who gets a name for early rising can stay in bed until midday.

It is a bad hen that does not scratch herself.

Mere words do not feed the friars.

Unwillingness easily finds an excuse.

The work praises the man. Two thirds of the work is the semblance.

When fire is applied to a stone it cracks.

Lose an hour in the morning and you'll be looking for it all day.

Laziness is a heavy burden.

Poverty waits at the gates of idleness.

Irish Proverbs
YOUTH & OLD AGE

As the big hound is, so will the pup be.

Age is honorable and youth is noble.

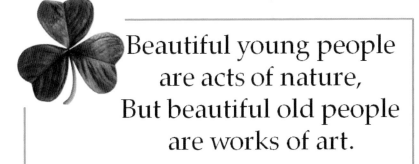

Beautiful young people
are acts of nature,
But beautiful old people
are works of art.

Youth does not mind where it sets its foot.

Time is a great story teller.

An old broom knows the dirty corners best.

The old person is a child twice.

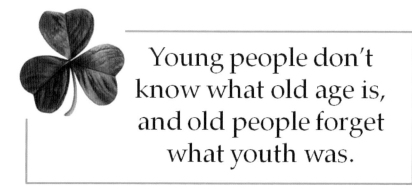

Young people don't know what old age is, and old people forget what youth was.

Praise the ripe field not the green corn.

The schoolhouse bell sounds bitter in youth and sweet in old age.

Youth sheds many a skin. The steed does not retain its speed forever.

The older the fiddle the sweeter the tune.

As the old cock crows, the young cock learns.

The old dog for the hard road and leave the pup on the path.

Irish Proverbs
LIFE'S UPS & DOWNS

There's nothing so bad that it couldn't be worse.

Life is a strange lad.

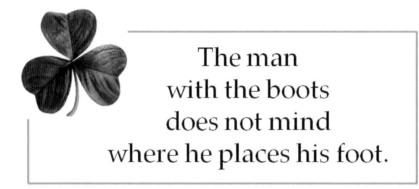

The man
with the boots
does not mind
where he places his foot.

If God sends you down a stony path, may he give you strong shoes.

It's an ill wind that blows nobody good.

However long the day, night must fall.

You must take the little potato with the big potato.

You cannot make a silk purse out of a sow's ear.

Three diseases without shame: Love, itch and thirst.

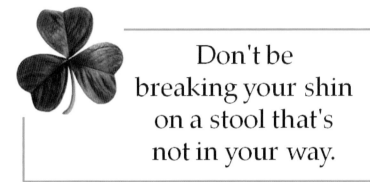

Don't be
breaking your shin
on a stool that's
not in your way.

It is better to exist unknown to the law.

Even a small thorn causes festering.

One must pay health its tithe.

If you move old furniture it may fall to bits.

Get down on your knees and thank God you're still on your feet.

A hen is heavy when carried far.

Irish Proverbs
ROMANCE & MARRIAGE

It's easy to halve the potato where there's love.

If you want praise, die. If you want blame, marry.

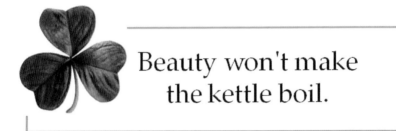

Beauty won't make the kettle boil.

You must live with a person to know a person. If you want to know me come and live with me.

Two shorten the road.

There is no fireside like your own fireside.

People live in each other's shelter.

Marriages are all happy. It's having breakfast together that causes all the trouble.

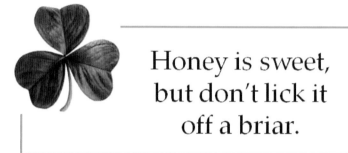

Honey is sweet, but don't lick it off a briar.

It's why women marry - the creatures, God bless them, are too shy to say no.

A whistling woman and a crowing hen will bring no luck to the house they are in.

You can't kiss an Irish girl unexpectedly. You can only kiss her sooner than she thought you would.

If you want to be criticized, marry.

Don't show your skin to a person who won't cover it.

A man cannot grow rich without his wife's leave.

Galway Bay

Irish Proverbs
FORTUNE & WEALTH

Enough and no waste is as good as a feast.

Cut your coat according to your cloth.

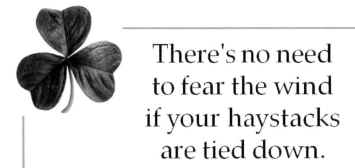

There's no need
to fear the wind
if your haystacks
are tied down.

He who has water and peat on his own farm has the world his own way.

A cat can look at a king.

It is not the same to go to the king's house as to come from it.

The life of an old hat is to cock it.

If you give the loan of your britches, don't cut off the buttons.

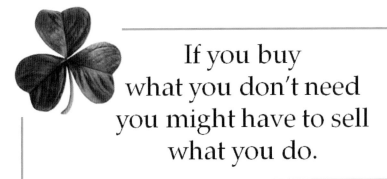

If you buy
what you don't need
you might have to sell
what you do.

It's not a matter of upper and lower class but of being up a while and down a while.

Lack of resource has hanged many a person.

The man who pays the piper calls the tune.

There never came a gatherer but a scatterer came after him.

Better be sparing at first than at last.

Hunger is a good sauce.

A heavy purse makes a light heart.

Heaven's leac na teine (stone before the fire) is reserved for the poor.

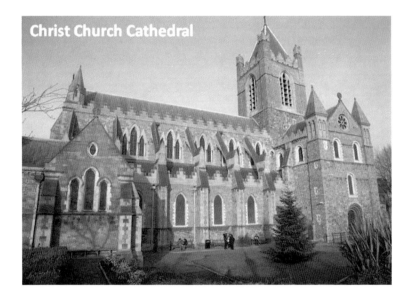

Christ Church Cathedral

Irish Proverbs
THE WISDOM OF SILENCE

Silence is the fence around the haggard where wisdom is stacked.

Melodious is the closed mouth.

Who keeps
his tongue
keeps his friends.

It is the quiet pigs that eat the meal.

Quiet people are well able to look after themselves.

Dingle Peninsula

Irish Proverbs
OBSERVATIONS ON LIFE

Questioning is the door of knowledge.

Necessity knows no law.

The river is no wider from this side than the other.

Need teaches a plan.

Burning the candle at both ends will soon leave you without a light.

God prefers prayers to tears.

Necessity is the mother of invention.

There is hope from the sea, but none from the grave.

There is no need like the lack of a friend.

There is no strength without unity.

Seldom is the last of anything better than the first.

Laughter is brightest, in the place here the food is.

Earth has no sorrows that heaven cannot heal.

It's difficult to choose between two blind goats.

The man with a cow doesn't need a scythe.

Every finger has not the same length, nor every son the same disposition.

Every branch blossoms according to the root from which it sprung.

They are scarce of news that speak ill of their mother.

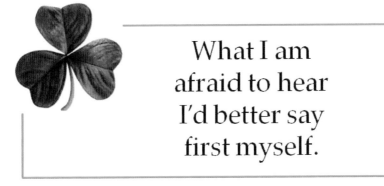

What I am afraid to hear I'd better say first myself.

Many a day shall we rest in the clay.

He who can follow his own will is a king.

Better fifty enemies outside the house than one within.

Put silk on a goat, and it's still a goat.

The smallest thing outlives the human being.

A lock is better than suspicion.

Wide is the door of the little cottage.

It is not a secret if it is known by three people.

BLESSINGS

Traditional Irish Blessings offer messages of hope, comfort, support and joy; here are three from my book *IRISH BLESSINGS - Over 100 Irish Blessings in 8 Categories*:

*May good luck be your friend
In whatever you do.
And may trouble be always
A stranger to you.*

May you have food and raiment,
A soft pillow for your head,
May you be forty years in heaven
Before the devil knows you're dead.

May your day be touched
by a bit of Irish luck,
brightened by a song in your heart,
and warmed by the smiles
of the people you love.

MORE IRISH

From Author Jean LeGrand
Available from Amazon.com and other retialers

BONUS

Here is a recipe for "Irish Cream Cupcakes" from my book *IRISH TREATS - 30 Dessert Recipes for St. Patrick's Day or Whenever You Want to Celebrate Like the Irish*.

These cupcakes get rave reviews from everybody who tries 'em ... I'm sure you and your family and friends will enjoy them, too.

24 servings

Total Time: 45 minutes
Prep Time: 25 minutes
Cook Time: 20 minutes + cooling

Ingredients:

½ cup butter, softened
1-½ cups granulated white sugar
2 eggs
3/4 cup unsweetened applesauce
2 tsp vanilla extract
2-½ cups all-purpose flour
3 tsp baking powder
½ tsp salt
½ cup Irish cream liqueur
Frosting:
1/3 cup butter, softened
4 ounces cream cheese (reduced-fat OK)
6 Tbs Irish cream liqueur
4 cups confectioners' sugar

Instructions:

1. Preheat oven to 350°F

2. Put pleated paper cupcake cups into two 12-cup muffin tins

3. In a medium bowl, sift together the flour, baking powder and salt, set aside

4. In a large bowl, beat butter and sugar until crumbly (about 2 minutes)

5. One at a time, add the eggs; beat well after each egg

6. Beat in applesauce and vanilla (mixture may appear curdled)

7. Gradually add the flour/baking soda/salt mixture and liqueur to the creamed mixture (butter, sugar, eggs); mix thoroughly ... alternate between adding the flour/baking soda/salt mixture and the liqueur, beating well after each addition

8. Fill paper-lined muffin cups two-thirds full

9. Bake at 350° for 18-22 minutes. Test for doneness: insert a toothpick near the center, if it comes out clean, the cake is ready

10. Cool for 10 minutes before removing from pans to wire racks to cool completely.

11. In a large mixing bowl, beat butter and cream cheese until fluffy

12. Beat liqueur into the butter/cream cheese mixture

13. Add confectioners' sugar to the butter/cream cheese/liqueur and beat until smooth

14. Spread or pipe the frosting over tops of thoroughly cooled cupcakes

These cupcakes are delicious, and you'll find 30 more great recipes in *Irish Treats* including:

> Desserts using Irish whiskey like: *Irish Whiskey Spice Cake* and *Irish Coffee Pie*
>
> Desserts using Irish stout like: *Classic Guinness Cake* and *Stout Floats*
>
> Fruit Dessert like: *Kerry Apple Tart* and *Apple Barley Pudding*
>
> Cookie & Cookie Bar Desserts like: *Blarney Stones* and *Triple Layer Irish Mint Brownies*

Candy Recipes like: *Yellowman Sponge Toffee* and *Irish Potatoes Candy*

Chocolate Desserts like: *Chocolate Meringue Bread Pudding* and *Chocolate Guinness Cake*

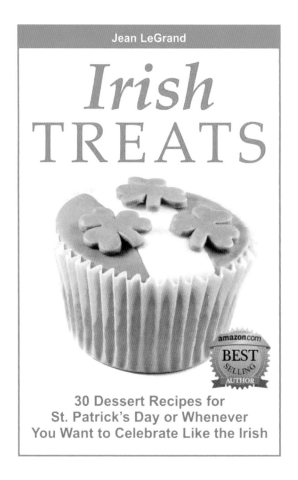

Available from Amazon.com and other retailers.

Can I Ask a Favor?

Thank you so much for reading my book. I hope you really liked it.

As you probably know, many people look at the reviews on Amazon before they decide to purchase a book.

If you liked this book, could you **please take a minute to leave a review** with your feedback?

Just go to Amazon.com, look up *Irish Proverbs - Jean LeGrand*, go to the book's page, then scroll down until you see the orange "Write a customer review button", click it and write a few words about why you like the book.

 A couple of minutes is all I'm asking for, and it would mean the world to me.

Thank you so much,

Jean

PHOTO CREDITS

Dedication Irish Uilleann Pipes-Full Set 1 January 2000 Own work **Ganainm** This file is licensed under the **Creative Commons Attribution 3.0 Unported** license.

Character & Honor_ Farad lighthouse, County Donegal, Ireland **karenwithak** **http://www.flickr.com/photos/moonrising/87446620/** This file is licensed under the **Creative Commons Attribution 2.0 Generic** license.

Opportunity The stunning Belfast Castle taken from the gardens. A very photogenic building which can be hired out for various events. 11 October 2009, 14:40 **Belfast Castle, Northern Ireland Andrew Hurley** from Wallasey, England, United Kingdom This file is licensed under the **Creative Commons Attribution-Share Alike 2.0 Generic** license.

Human Nature View of Baltimore Beacon near Baltimore, Co. Cork, Ireland. 1 July 2008 Self-taken photo of structure in public place Ben Rudiak-Gould **public domain**

Patience Ireland 2009, Clonmacnoise castle ruins 8 August 2009, 17:13:49 originally posted to **Flickr** as **Ireland 2009, Clonmacnoise castle ruins Kevin King** This file is licensed under the **Creative Commons Attribution 2.0 Generic** license.

Stupidity Leprechaun Crossing **Neil and Kathy Carey** Neil and Kathy Carey Member **May 22, 2004 Canon PowerShot A40** This file is licensed under the **Creative Commons Attribution-Share Alike 2.0 Generic** license.

Wisdom Dublin Castle **William Murphy** infomatique **May 15, 2005 Sigma SD9** This file is licensed under the **Creative Commons Attribution-Share Alike 2.0 Generic** license.

Drinking Old Ireland House 30 August 2005 Own work Umberto Fistarol This file is licensed under the **Creative Commons Attribution 3.0 Unported** license and under the terms of the **GNU Free Documentation License**, Version 1.2 or any later version published by the **Free Software Foundation**; with no Invariant Sections, no Front-Cover Texts, and no Back-Cover Texts.

Advice Ivy growing on the national university of Galway building, Ireland **Martie Swart** martie1swart **August 17, 2009 Galway, Galway, IE Canon EOS 500D** This file is licensed under the **Creative Commons Attribution 2.0 Generic** license.

Work & Idleness Clonmacnoise View of the River Shannon with one of the round towers. Much of the low lying areas were under water, despite this being nearly the end of June. 19 June 1981 From **geograph.org.uk Alan Murray-Rust** This file is licensed under the **Creative Commons Attribution-Share Alike 2.0 Generic** license.

Youth & Old Age One of the **Carrowmore** tombs in **Ireland**. June 6, 2002, Canon D60 camera. Photographer Jon Sullivan **http://pdphoto.org/PictureDetail.php?mat=pdef&pg=6015** 6 September 2004 (original upload date) - Date of photo per source 17 June 2002 Original source page **http://pdphoto.org/PictureDetail.php?mat=&pg=6015** Transferred from **en.wikipedia**; transferred to Commons by **User:Wadester16** using **CommonsHelper**. Original uploader was **Sverdrup** at **en.wikipedia** *This image from PD Photo.org has been released into the public domain by its author and copyright holder, Jon Sullivan.*

Life's Ups & Downs_ Connemara **Olivier Bruchez** Olivier Bruchez **August 8, 2011 Screeb, Galway, IE Casio EX-Z1080** This file is licensed under the **Creative Commons Attribution-Share Alike 2.0 Generic** license.

Romance & Marriage_ Ireland Galway-Bay **Michael Bertulat** M. Bertulat **August 26, 2007** This file is licensed under the **Creative Commons Attribution 2.0 Generic** license.

Fortune & Wealth_ Christ Church Cathedral, Dublin 7 December 2008, 14:16:57 originally posted to **Flickr** as **Christchurch Cathedral – Dublin William Murphy** This file is licensed under the **Creative Commons Attribution-Share Alike 2.0 Generic** license.

The Wisdom of Silence_ Slea Head from Dunbeg Fort, Dingle Peninsula, Kerry, Ireland. 7 September 2007, 11:15:55 originally posted to **Flickr** as **Slea Head from Dunbeg Fort, Dingle Peninsula, Kerry, Ireland Jim** This file is licensed under the **Creative Commons Attribution 2.0 Generic** license.

Observations on Life_ Green Road near Lisdoonvarna, Co. Clare, Ireland April 1989 **Sludge G** sludgegulper Member since 2008 Taken on **October 13, 2010** This file is licensed under the **Creative Commons Attribution-Share Alike 2.0 Generic** license

12153386R10033

Made in the USA
San Bernardino, CA
12 June 2014